A Point
Is That
Which
Has No
Part

Winner of the 2000
James Laughlin Award
of The Academy of
American Poets

The James Laughlin
Award is given to commend
and support a poet's second book.
The only award of its kind in the
United States, it is named in honor
of the poet and publisher James
Laughlin (1914–1997), who founded
New Directions in 1936. The award
is endowed by a gift to The Academy
of American Poets from the Drue
Heinz Trust.

JUDGES FOR 2000
Agha Shahid Ali
Lynn Emanuel
Marilyn Nelson

A Point Is That Which Has No Part

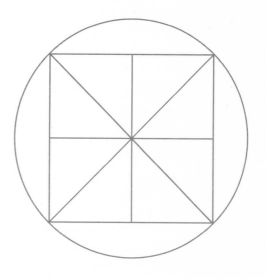

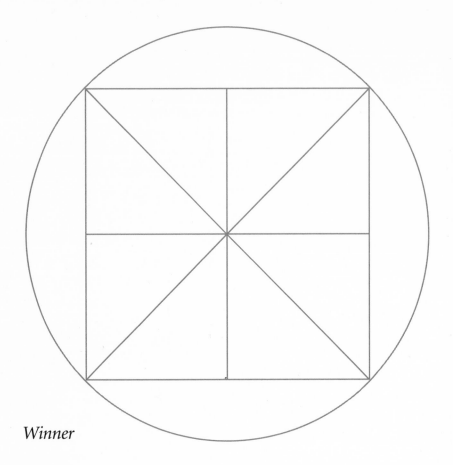

Winner

of the

Iowa

Poetry

Prize

A Point Is That Which Has No Part

Poems by

Liz Waldner

University of Iowa Press

Iowa City

University of Iowa Press, Iowa City 52242

Printed in the United States of America
Design by Richard Hendel
http://www.uiowa.edu/~uipress
This cloth edition was published as the James Laughlin Award
edition for The Academy of American Poets in 2001.

Printed on acid-free paper
Library of Congress Cataloging-in-Publication Data
Waldner, Liz.
    A point is that which has no part: poems / by Liz Waldner.
        p.   cm. (The Iowa poetry prize)
    ISBN 0-87745-751-4
        I. Title.   II. Series.
    PS3473.A42158   P65   2000
    811'.54—dc21   99-056175

Circles and right lines

limit and close all bodies,

and the mortal right-lined

circle, must conclude and

limit all.

—Sir Thomas Browne

Contents

Acknowledgments

"Radioactive Assay and Epitaph (Indian School)": *New American Writing*; "Accord": *Phoebe*; "A Very Big Wind": *Talisman*; "Talented and Gifted," "Dialogum," "Wednesday Morning Pray Time": *Tinfish*; "Everything But": *Woodstock Center For Photography Journal, Key Satch(el)*; "Trading Little Trinkets with the Gods": *No Roses Review*; "Sufficient Causes and Artifacts": *Poet's Calendar, Rooms*; "Interruptus," "Of Unknowing Again": *First Intensity*; "The Tree-Keeper's Daughter Speaks," "Self-Representation," "Maundy Thursday in Translation": *Denver Quarterly*; "Where, Broken (the darkness)": *Colorado Review*; "Boom Profits of Doom": *Kenning*; "*Au Pair* a green": *Massachusetts Review*; "'Under the Tinsel There Is the Real Tinsel'": *6ix*; "Misses Coordinates (old world mail order)," "Welling," "Mission Control": *Litrag*; "Flight Path of Real Desires (my sister visits on the astral plane)": *American Letters & Commentary*; "Fear and Suckling and the Mirroring unto Death," "The Laundress Maunders II": *Capilano Review*; "The Dinner Date": *Volt*; "The Scientific Method": *Malahat Review*.

Thanks also to the Massachusetts Cultural Council, Djerassi, Centrum, Villa Montalvo, and the Vermont Studio Center.

i. POINT

A point is that which has no part.

—Euclid's *Elements*, Definition 1

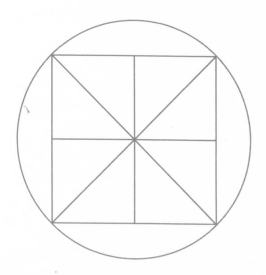

Accord

Sticks stick up out of the brittle leaves the leather color of winter oak. A donkey trundles its burden of cordwood and hock. Seeds arabesque a stalk, describing the shapes of Farsi to those who have eyes to hear. I'm not one, but I know what it's like. It's like here comes a shadow, the sun on my ankle, all the body's weight on my poor old ass. Jesus rode an ass into Jerusalem where the people waved palms. I wave my palm and a wind rises fast. So far I'm happy with this arrangement; I only hope it lasts.

ii. LINE

A line is breadthless length.

—Definition 2

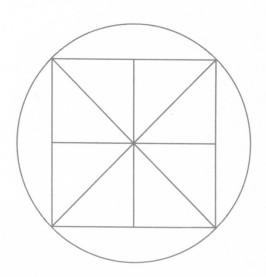

Straight Flush

For behold, I have graven thee on the palms of my hands.—Isaiah

The hand, the hand of the man who sat on my couch and held whatever I put in his hands, sands, soap-operatic voice declaims *of time*, mere weeks before they steer the wheel of his car away. We're west here, there's steers, away is farther than you think and here NO, NO's another Thing Not To Say, along with "Hello, excuse and pardon me, but sitting beside you at the movie, I chanced to smell your breath and swooned to taste your mouth." Meanwhile—and it *was* mean, being the cause of great shiftings about in my seat and a general chill in limbs deserted by blood all gone with its heat to the libido's seat—meanwhile he sat arms crossed and wouldn't look. At me, I mean, wondering if I'd attained instantaneous status as Open Book, radiating pheremones in the body's matter-of-fact tongues, translating Golden Mean to Golden Rule: yearn transfixedly for the hands of others as you would have them yearn for the hands of you. Tanked up on Eros, beauty's petrol (a seabird indicating Aphrodite's ocean is near— with another, a noetic Noah, hoping the heavens will open), a high-octane fuel, first choice of any Fool one foot on the cliff-lip, ready to leap the distance between his hand holding smoking hand-rolled, my hand holding matches from The Palm Broker: seal Fate's deal with a handshake? Mine shakes; hard to keep your parts in their seats late night in the kitchen: he's there there, I'm here here here handing calling cards out, saying: I'm out, out upon it three whole days, as John Donne or Sir Suckling or somebody like unto it says. Saying, "Excuse, hillo, pardon but I can no longer bear not touching you, I must needs away to the big window to hang my headed-for-archaic torso out like laundry in the night air and you must needs leave (O perish quickly the untoward thought) so I can exhale without speech."

Upon which, small a prayer and all head, no-hearter as it was, bad god heard and answered, for the man of the hand upped and awayed to sleep, saying he'd better get some and he thought he knew where, so I got none, instead pacing a curious figure on the carpet, hands held over my face, feeling my way through old cue cards engraved there, trying out *selfish*, trying out *weak*; rehearsing how it is kind not to say Things Not To Say and rehearsing how needful it is to speak.

Where Credit Is Due (Do You Know the Way to San Jose?)

To speak. So to speak. Of Steven's Creek, home to six streams of cars flowing between monolithic Home Depot and its mausoleum-like clones, cliff faces of waste spaces, mauled, strip-malled for miles, as far as the eye can see, which isn't far at all in such smog. The eye smarts, the smart-ass I, the one the squirrel scolds when I get up cold after my two hours of sleep, and the stellar jay hollers at me. Apologetically, I show them my credit cards, sitting also cold and thin beneath the morning tree saying: shiny, pretty, I believe you like these? Skinnier than I can afford to be, not from making payments regularly but from paying over-dues. Brought to account: up all night because I can't afford not to be. Sleeping expensively, waking frugally: no transition time from "out of it" to right back in where we left off last night: you stand angling for words and I balance on a wor(l)dless corner of the couch, the davenport, port authority, part alterity: if I touch what you say is heir to break, I fear the house of cards we build of air between us falls apart. The heart in the kitchen dark after reproves: *mercy is more than the rules.*

To speak or not to speak, that is the question I pay interest on. Can I handle the payments? The poet one couldn't handle me, the priest one broke my handles off, the one with the hands—we'll have to watch and see. Sea change. Loose change. What comes loose? "I" from "me"? "Thou" from "thee"? The computer refuses to process these words, announcing: Insufficient File Handles to Run WP. Unprocessedly, at any rate (the interest here's high), he's good (for it, good as his word, amor-tizing the worst effects of Pep Boys, Bloomingdale's, Barnes & Noble's, For Eyes—all chains and shackles demanding we should synthesize desire) company, which isn't all I ever claim to need but what the traffic now will bear. So to speak.

Ear Rational (watercourse for tongues of flame)

Bear: not to moan as you say to the audience, *and this piece an erotics of speech.* Ear: through the nights and through the days, the sound of water, *and darkness was on the face of the deep.* To tremble in the breath of. To hear the heart beat. *The beauty of the green earth, the mystery of the waters, the white moon among the stars.* How I wonder what you are *as I wander out under the sky . . .*

I listen to you through the walls, hear through a glass, darkly; you crack open your bedroom window to the creek—*the better to hear you with, my dear*: an erotics of hear here. *And Being, but an Ear,* I become your body arriving in waves, your palm sliding in its tide the length of my thigh, my listening skin. Listening in: breath, the sound of the invisible ocean's waves by night. Waved palms as he entered into Jerusalem. Salem, Mass.; home to witches, of which you think me one. Still? Late of Mass., my name means "house of God." Yours is that of a prophet, without honor in your own country for having entered into mine. *In the mines, in the mines, in the Blue Diamond mines, I worked my life away, O fall on your knees and pray* your witch survives her trip to the under-world via the ducking stool; the pond is already deep—go ask Alice, who swam in her tears, too, when she was no longer ten feet tall. If I drown I am innocent and may have lived; if I float I am damned. *The Days Of Our Lives. As The World Turns.* An equally problematic soap, Ivory, 99 and 99/100 percent pure, floats—and microwaved, billows out cumulous clouds to rain its own trial by flood.

I would not be a trial by fire for you. Forgive my fire its flame. It is all that I am. In my house there are many mansions, and in each a candle burns for you. If you didn't light them, who? *Where is the way where light dwellest? And as for darkness, where is its place that thou should know the paths to its house?* Its deep house where, in each deep window, a flame broods over its double. Reflection: she, candle in a dark room, stands before her window having fled, having said she couldn't handle *the marks of the ancient flame.* Poor Dido, I knew her well (wherein she drowned). Her forfeit kingdom by the sea. *O I was a child and she was a child in our kingdom by the sea, and the angels above envied the love . . .*

We are not altogether unenviable in our unkingdom by the creek; having abdicated, our crowns are ciphers, as Lear's fool well knew. Zero, the world's egg, from which the alchemical Sun is born; the place-holder, the no-place-made yet. *After the final no there comes a yes / And on that yes the future world depends. / No was the night. Yes is this present sun.* May our unkingdom come to this. Doubtful but not doused . . . Dowse for the held place with a willow wand. I'll call that your hand. With it, lead me beside the still waters for your name's sake. I can't say your staff it comforts me, but it makes me cry *faith* with a mouth long closed. *Reach hither thy finger and behold my hands. Reach hither thy hand and thrust it into my side.* I open wide. Thomas doubts what's dead can rise. I doubt what rises is allowed to be alive. And I believe; *help thou mine unbelief.*

What rises. The sun in my breast for you. By day so bright, at night so burned I could not see that *In every place on which the sun sees the water, the water also sees the sun and in each of these places it can present the sun's image to the eye*: Da Vinci's *Opticks* alchemizes (*tertium non datus*, but implied); beats Newton's (and its two-body problems) all to hell. The damned (again)(splash). The doomed. You invite me to see star-crossed lovers on the silvery-moon screen, spoon, June, spleen. Paris. Achilles. My own heel scraped by the entrance gate. Gatekeepers: Montague, Capulet, integument, internment, interment—and on the third day, rose again. *A rose by any other name would smell as sweet.* Let's call this a law of nature, having the "force of law." *Whether law is something pertaining to reason? Objection 1. It would seem that law is not something pertaining to reason.* St. Thomas goes on (and on) to prove this wrong, but it is right. Being and Seeming, the slippage, the catch. *Canst thou draw out Leviathan with an hook?* Fishers of men: awful St. Paul to the Romans: I see another law in my members. Yes, well, our membership begun outside some law, but not all; it depends on where you begin, which thread you trust to follow out of the maze. Even "A is for Adam in whom sinned we all" can get you to law and law to punish, Panopticon, Satyricon, the garden Pan (the bread of life), the Villa lawn, how does your garden grow? Rosemary is for remembrance, and it's everywhere here. You speak of your in-laws and think of your wife; the sun sees the water suffer and suffers along. Silent. I don't flinch; not in this for a quick dip but the long run with you: creek bed below sings you to sleep all day after all night awake in a similar bed. Slipstream (*could I slip in beside you?* and the sun rises in the night), a river of words and a rock of silence it spills and splits around until you pull me down to swim. The deeps. *Ichthys,* the secret fish a sign of meeting. "Kitty-fish": other lines, lives, other houses, other mazes, the eclipse of my Meow, another channel opened now. We met, we meet. The flick of a fin.

Finis: fate. Ponder, wonder, wander. The river Lysander. Today's a meander. Terrible weather for the day-after: dank, grey, danker fear you'll go away. Curled up in separate beds to meet again where time has pooled *again.* I pool in you? You pool in me. See? Look in, your face is in me. See "the sun's image," a face with a calyx of flames aswim. See your own "in each of these places." See the sun see the water, and the I's therein.

Sun Dial

Call him up! Call him up! Jesus is on the line.

Therein a bed, they are. One supposes that the other doesn't notice they're not supposed to be; however, she does more than notice. She feels what she sees. I speak here of me, who is not a girl in a T-shirt with flappy hair heading for her car over there without a coat. It's cold here where there's sun after so many days of grey to rain that doesn't always come. Words, neither. Maybe it's too much to expect answers to questions about pain from the one turning burning smoked on the spit. Shit. This isn't going anywhere, never mind in circles; I've joined you, you just don't know: like a ham from the rafters, I hang upside down, trussed—the tarot's Hanged One my template, the card of "sacrifice, surrender, seeing unconventionally"—I dangle by one ankle, twist in the wind, pendant on a string, bound by the cord of my desire. Ham I Am. Last supper, illumination, halo wearer, an era in which the head was called the pate. *Upon which one may play knick knack paddywhack, give the dog a bone* (a pretty dog he says, and thinks of who's walking his own), *this old man came rolling home.* What old man? He's young, and younger. And he swims like a fish in the spring of himself and he feeds on hunger. Pleasure he suspects of being his undoing. I suspect we are made to be undone, again and again, until love teaches suffer its name. No is the O, the concentric; how to open the O, undo the easy-for-me round of Renounce? The dead one said: For some, Lent is renunciation; for others, embrace. He didn't know how, either. O breach, preach, pleach, fruit tree, cross of the knee, crown of thorns, we are made to be (what we) desire. Its fire is to burn away the clock hands the mind hires to tick us off and away. Away, stay, O, for that country with a pond. O for twenty years gone. Gone: a fly hops his shadow from the husk of a leaf to the crust of a centipede with a mustache of brittle feet. Scan: al*right*, al*right*, our flesh is as grass; our days, the hairs of our head, numbered, pass. Numbers become numb: calculate production and deployment of paychecks, dividends of pain, debt, guilt, grief, obligation. No: to hide behind obligation. To count the cost of personal forms of nerve gas. Impasse: can not go, can not stay: the sun burns an extra moment in the day:

apogee: its very shadow burns away. Invention: noon on sun dial (=faint but perceptible belief in *not fade away*?), a thing congruent with itself, a thing to long for, single.

See how the bricks make the pediment up, how the chain's shadow on it doesn't have the chain's rust. At Hiroshima, these shadows burned right in, a moment's skin become the remaining gauge of a life. The measure of my days made by the shadow of your wife.

Mapper of (Possible) Fact

Wife of Bath, a model? Forsooth, single, however many times husbanded. For good measure, feather in her cap, this one and that, en route to prayer. Fletcher, worshipful company of. Finger, cold, gold, pearl of great price: single. Singlet, doublet, articles of clothing. But, conjunctive of loathing. Fear: I'll hear the night's No and undress anyway. Yes? Dress for excess; in rhyme, I'll try triplets. *Menage aux bois*: he cuts it, I grow it. Who throws it? Husband, wife—would it throw them for more useful loops (lassoo? lariat?) if I were a he? As ever, the wonder, as if I could be. If I were a man, I'd love you too. Still. Like me. Androgyny a matter of synergy—

But enough of single-lens reflexive anxiety (and speculation). I've a singular eye for beauty and it's yours (causation, absolute relation). What else is: the place of meeting which of course, perforce, is empty. Empty is enough. Is all: where did I touch while you drove the letterbox car through the streets? (How how you drive is how you love is another letter's labor.) My hand beneath your thigh upon the seat. Heat whence nothing was: a feat. Where felt? Heart's seat; moved even my knees in your direction while leaving poor feet on the floor. Who can compass such arrangements? Oh let go—go how you crouch in your seat and steer with your fists in your lap, easy. Drive by the seat of the pants—so to speak. Steer me some more. I would veer westerly—I would ride—I would go always at your side to be with you in your need—and mine—

Of Unknowing Again

. . . and why amongst all the clouds of the sky each itself and peculiar
I could not determine the sun.

Not mine. Could not. Some humped bug lumbers across the Formica-topped table, its front end pumped up as if speed-boating along, despite its lack of speed.

Is that a lesson? Parable? Parabola. Thrown for equidistant loops, boomeranged back to Begin Again. Go with fixed points, bring in John Donne's compass feet (six for insectual or meter's pleasures, heart's own iambs?) or throw in lot with conic sections? There find *con* with and *con* scam or comic; yes, conic: Apollonius, (sing antiphonal), another *knew him well*—

Could not. A letter writ me in praise of your wife's eyes. Mornings solo in the kitchenful of first light (insomniamb) and last night's bottles, glasses and cups of tea ("we have a beautiful cosmos, you and me . . ."), the formicary's output aswarm on that far Formica (February falling further and further behind in mid-April's wake (taxed, I attacks, I know)). Know well your body. Its shoulder range over me home. Wanted. Mined field. Scammed mine so to do, yet met, meet and right, in body's hand-trust. Meek mine shaft. Inherited d/earth, so write write write; would hand-right, but I can't tell the right story. Which perfect thing is right? I want—

Could not. You said so. I shone on just alike.

Could not. Come to this. A ha-ha god: you gave me my body and now it belongs to you. Where are you? I'm right behind your eyes. As when bend to see self in puddle and see sun instead: matter of belief. Here, far, they say of a mountain as if of the sun: *it's out.* Matter of fixed point, of view, and velocity, too (three). The count: I'm out. A matter of my seeing through (to) you.

Could not. Not be. Not known. Not me.

Self-identity—what else?
My hands held sudden and fast in your mouth.

iii. CIRCLE

To construct a circle with any

center and any distance.

—Postulate 3

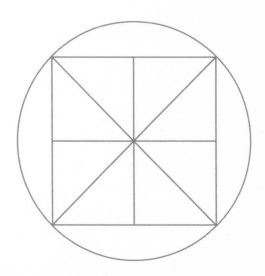

Hand to Mouth (Twist and Shout)

Cold comes slow up out
of the darkness among the leaves
that smell so good when bruised

Do you, too, recognize me
god so soon?

Her First Reckoning

Pour wine into vessels the violet of woods,
wine of the reddening stars.
You are god, you can do it.

Your lover calls you St. John the Conquerer.
I have heard her.
This is the name of a root.

Asperge the thousands and thousands of rooms
in which photosynthesis promises sun
to the acolyte cells. Rain yourself on a leaf.

Birch. The bark is malleable as mushroom flesh.
Show that you know me. Scratch out my name
with this tree. My name of trees.

On the day I arrive at the door of my death,
myself now hard to tell
from the trees that had hid it from me,

I will demand that you love me.
You made me like this.
Why did you make me like this?

Self-Representation

Wald–[German]: forest

How blurry the trees in these window reflections,
like pond water, the sky color, too.

I've been to Walden Pond.
I've been in Walden Pond.

This is one thing I write with ease;
the first half is the first half

of my name. The trees in it wave
past me, to someone too blurry to see.

Trees, inscribe me with me.
Let leaf be *to wound*

as word is to image. Let *me*
correspond with me.

I've never been to me.
I've never been in me.

But daily I rehearse
how I drowned.

The Tree-Keeper's Daughter Speaks

It is no good.
Rather IT is; I'm not.
Piece of paper on a shelf
wrinkled with a water stain.
I will never be myself.

A stone could never
have another
idea it ought to be
some other. I feel sadder
to think to be a stone.

Can a lifetime of wearing glasses
make you think the world is in a jar?

In the jar is water
and a paper
and a stone.

On the paper is a message
encouraging my guardian angel to try:
if they do such things in the green tree,
what shall be done in the dry?

The Alchemist's Misfortune

Hemlock branches shook their heads,
gently. I built a fire, lit a candle,
needed last night back.
Last night I needed now, this morning. How
the flames fly up like will.

The forest drips. The fog is what
I wished I were, the medium
of ether. Candle wax becomes the mind
of fire. Melting snow forgets and grows
foregone roadside rivers.

Hemlock needles scatter on the sill.
Too sad for good-bye as a party,
I went to bed alone and cried.
This morning packing boxes,
I've made myself not-matter.

Maundy Thursday in Translation

. . . after he had washed their feet . . . he said unto them,
Know ye what I have done to you?—John 13:12

Do you know what I have done to you?

In the woodstove, a fire of explosive smolders.
(This I deem a kind of consonant, like fricative only hotter.)

In the room made of trees, licking ashes from your jacket.
(This I call communion with the mat(t)er.)

In the bathhouse tub, my other mouth with other tongues.
(This the ark, this the covenant, this the living water.)

Melting pen in hand, I dirty page 12 with rivers-of-water ink.
Drink. Do you know what I have done to you?

In in in. You said, "At least
supply your own preposition."

I've done what you asked of me.
Of what I've done to you, the least.

If I wash thee not, thou hast no part with me.
(In my other's mouth, there are many scansions.)

In you, I drip from every leaf.

Au pair a green

All the bells say: too late. This is not for tears; thinking.—*John Berryman*

You could think of the new green as a sort of dirt on the trees at this point.
At this point I look in the mirror where I see I look like what I am:
stricken. What is cast over the sky when they call it overcast?
Tears (*not for thinking*) stitch soles'. Shoes.

It's true I am in love with your friend and not you? He got his body in first.
Some juice (I quote what I wrote at 16) is glue. I am going. I am
always going, but in this case, I was going to say: I am
going. To quit writing. (that juice)

But like Augustine, again, not yet. I love you and I want so slowly to
come to your touch that every learned thing's burned finger
print falls away. Today I understand all who
drive nails into their hands. Again.

Pfand. Perhaps there will be yet another German word from you
in my mailbox soon and I will go sleek between my legs and
my heart will lurch open and heat yet another short-term
room at whose end I will yet be. Alone?

By their doubts ye shall know them; never about that last a doubt. Re-
doubt: "Let us rest beneath the trees." Your friend calls me
by the name of a tree. Rest beneath me. It will rain
on us green and you will know what "it" means.

To last
to come   clean with me.

Transitive, Intransitive: Extemporary Measures

Two crows above the marsh: sew.
Stitch the seventeen sleek shades of blue
to the shadow-patterned greens below.
See fit to make me a suitable view who
having nowhere else to go
might as well wear this world well.
Llama necks periscope the view:
yonder, across the water, you
testing the air now a crow
chases a redwinged blackbird through.

What can I show you who sees
I don't believe? For now,
what the eye of the needle sees:
through through through:
clouds, birds, me, trees;
soon: *in, out, with, to*;
something moving, something moved:
a stitch in time's an avenue,
future's sutures' revenue—
"the shining hour" improved.

Fear and Suckling and the Mirroring unto Death

. . . Which alters when it alteration finds

Two calcium clouds have appeared in the sky
of my fourth finger's nail.
The fourth finger of my left hand means to me
the sound of the letter L.

As I write this L, a big wind blows
and leaves leave the trees sideways.
Trying to stay, I adjust my glasses.
I pour linden (the lost love's name for me)
honey and a Chinese herb into my tea and see
in its dark mirror the red-orange teeth
of the tiger lily dying in its day.
The mirror moves when my hand moves
and so do the teeth and the day.

I move when you move.
Take my hand and see.
Put my clouds in your mouth.
Still me.

Tell me this way
Love is not a talent.
Suck. Correct my vision.
Still me.

Where, Broken (the darkness

Cows on the spine of the hill like the spine of a book are some letters

Letters with legs; like an E and an L or an R that is squared like the box of the body of cows

Like the spine of a book, the legs and the bodies of cows spell out the name and maybe the head spells also the name of the book on whose spine is embossed the name made of grass:

The light of the many days and the darkness the roots of the grass pull up out of the hill and the light pushes down with the feet of the cows and the darkness inside of the skulls of the cows, all these the name has eaten

The lines of the spines of the cows grazing the sky, the meeting of spine and sky also marking the arcing edges of dark or light letters on dark or light pages where, broken, the name grazes the thing it will know or mean or become

These are the choices.
However, there *are* other books.

is named) Orpheus

Music, for instance.

In this instance, editions of one moment tenacious and tough as the roots of the grass; foxing of foxes, errata of light, elegiacal lyre of the hair of the hill, hylation, length of reed and duration. The sky's undulation, corralling the contours of gold and green's vibration, a range of texts, a library home home on the range.

Run your eyes over the spines of the books, sound out the vertabrae: musics issue. Current issue, brook of days, yet made of *broken / here / the names*—as Stonehenge is broken: some ratios eroded away. Some seconds, some teeth are missing; a molar, a mortar, a moment to grind out the day, sounds the name itself has worn away. Now the mouth can't pronounce itself; in this way, becomes its own shadow.

In this instance, fullness of darkness. In this finds an angle, a pitch away from mute. One note held: recognition. The hand of the mind reaches—and fails. The golden light of intervals silent. The Impenetrable bruises the in-between. The echo the look of Eurydice's loss: say *I want* and see *I want* become so clear you pass right through . . .

The cattle gather around a welling of loss, the underworld's access to the upper world's web. They drink from a limpid eye full of sky. Read here what you will: sad face, lost skin still on the hoof, a hill rilled with a word made of cows, a jawbone still-toothed incised against the sky, chewing the meaning's echo, little wave on the water, the name's immortal but scored good-bye.

iV. SQUARE

A straight line is that which lies evenly

with all the points on itself.

—Definition 4

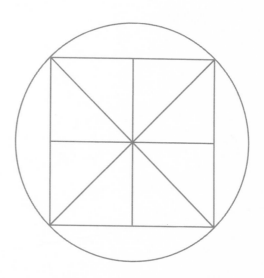

A Very Big Wind

I dreamed a tornado. White-glove affair (no dust, no muss, *ich muss*, ichthys, fly fish, Icarus: look, pa, no hands nor flies on me) interrupted by this spinny missive from the heavens. National Weather Service mythology: Gods' messenger, Iris, spreads wings, lifts weights: isobars at god's gym with her homeys, The Fates. "Gymnopedies," metronome, music of now eerie spheres, "spears" is how you say that in Mississippi, where Zeus, ever handy with a caduceus, pierces the skies with his thunderbolts, screws up a few things, sends us a slinky of wind to tuck us in, or tuck into us, as the case may be—in any case, once again, a very big wind. And the fish rises to the flicked fly: alas, poor Icarus, he flew so well. The thunder rumbles across the river in, yep, the Catskills. Washington Irving or Julius, bowling balls or basket, beltway or Orion's belt, in a democracy we choose our heavens and our dearths, too, thereby. And here I set (not a hen, just southern), watching the trees' green ravishing, the wind moving them like you move me although I mostly only yearn to show my name means tree. Limbs long enough, eh?—but boned, excuse the expression. They, trees, meanwhile chant those names the druids knew before they became a major league team—and demonstrate that what the bird flew through is theirs, too: anything that moves you is, and helps you know your name. What does the tongue of tornado seek as licking, licking, this way it comes? More, more. Knowledge of houses, sex with the trees. The fish rises to the flicked fly's and yours to my need.

Talented and Gifted

He hurt her amateur feelings. No bandages, please. A panda bear from the county fair is like unto a spelling error: Ouch, delete on bended knee. Pedigrees not withstanding on their greasy feet (O blue blood, O 10w40, O lubricated with nonoxynol, O engine engine #9, how doth thy corporate chassis shine, $$$ maketh the world to turn, you _____ my _____ and I'll _____ thine), pigeon is a language spoken by all who puffeth themselves up, causing their chest parts to go before them as pride goeth before a fall. An economics Just-So Story, brought to you by the makers of Geritol. Hi kids. Can you say Black Monday? Forced retirement? Over-inflated? The market is a little bit nervous, the market has the jitters, the market has an Excedrin headache: no futures trading tonight, dear. No nonoxynol necessary; the fruits of his labor land in a little wad of the financial section while she sniffles in the next room. He sleeps, snores, stretches, thumbs through the coffee table volume of *The Sexual Parts of Plants.* Geez Louise, who framed such fearsome symmetries? Faithful dog noses his crotch for her head to be petted. O dog (he pets), you really are clairvoyant and a relative of god. Make that <u>mature</u> feelings.

Mission Control

Well, we are doing the best we have with what we can or something to that effect. Here he comes, there he goes, hands in pockets, swivel from the hip, O hip hooray, O Big Mac and the midriff crisis. The Mid-Atlantic Rift. Riffle goes the water of life. Ruffles have ridges, great. We just persist, we try, we try. This is very trying. The roof of the mouth, the mountains of the moon, more ridges. He fidgets. She budgets. They diet. There's Nutri-Slim-Fast Discover Cards. There's lift-off stains and everything. Everything's OK.

Housewife's Lament

Here I am. Sam I am. Not Spam. Nor Pam, an awful name for another awful product. Blame. Lame. Negativity abounds. He'll say PMS makes the rounds. I do feel mean as a snake skinned. Once I was finned; before it did it, it looked me in the eye. It, the fish. Wife, wish. A kiss, a load of laundry, the washer in the faucet, the hinge in the wrist, the watcher in the clock face, impermanent wave tryst. Improbable. Bubble. Scheme burst. Scene 2, in which Artaud is advised he wears his volume oh so loud. Turn down that damn heart off. With a bristle bristle here and a bristle bristle there = our masculine ego has suffered some more. Repeat after me, I am a bore. Copy this 500 times. Nobody heard of carpal tunnel syndrome In Those Days. In the days of the bee sips from the leaf tip, the scent of minted air. Meanwhile, somewhere, etc. The relative humidity is 90 percent, the temperature 92. (One must never say *temp*, it is disgusting, like Pam.) Large statistics are in my brain. I don't even want your goddam kiss, mister plumber. Let's see if you have the sense to keep on walking. No, it appears you do not, which is a pity. You have no kind of humility. Except I bet with your mother but that's hardly relative. It's always the Me Show with you, or is that me? It's that volume knob again, transposes the brain waves of even the lowliest of reptiles, I gotta tell you and you, for all your racket, aren't going to be able to hear. Big sigh and irritations. If only I owned my own home.

Everything But

What, vhat, I always want the words out faster because I can feel the press of more to say. I can also feel the press of this question not content to rest at the back of my mind: does anybody know why ice—the kind of giant frozen waterfall of ice you pass on the Mass Pike cut, for instance—has that unearthly Aqua Velva color? Something to do with wave lengths, no doubt, but I forget whether things absorb the frequency of the color they appear or everything but it. Still, why should ice be that weird blue nothing else natural is? Well, is anything anything else's color? Who knows? This seems a decent place to end our inquiry for the a.m., although I had looked forward to writing about my visit to Mammoth Caves, Kentucky, when I was eleven and had baby-blue cat-eye prescription sunglasses because my regular ones broke and how like stalactites are the ice falls on the Mass Pike and how in the caves they give the formations names and the people thought I was blind and whispered, *Shh*, when we came to the underground river where the blind fish live, giving me a name like so. Uh-oh, everyone but me is done with their childhoods and I didn't get to ask if they still make Aqua Velva. Who are They? Where did They go? I have no *album de photo*, only a mental file whose directory is an assemblage of optometric icons, a chronology of discarded glasses frames, *removed as it were to some inner place, which is yet no place.* My eyes bigger than my belly: as Augustine also said, it is as if the memory were the belly of the soul: *A large and boundless chamber! Whoever sounded the bottom thereof?* The vast, the deep, the feeling of 1969 imprisoned in baby-blue plastic imprisoned in the only photo of that time. The genie released by the blue of ice or the taste, yes, of madeleine. The things we absorb—when I close my eyes, I can see me eleven again, me doing dishes in the kitchen sink, the light isn't light enough, my father's brain is preparing his death, on the TV a sexy woman voice is singing *there's something about an Aqua Velva man*—but I wouldn't be if you paid me.

This Is Not Normal Movements of the Animal Kingdom

OK, here we go, yes. Press. Again? For time? No? For space? No? For they are the same out in such snow? Brilliant. Whell, which typo (handwrit nonetheless) reminds me of the shell whelk is, but I mean well, what on earth was I going to say? (Good intentions, Dante's Hell this cold, ah so.) And after this little disquisition? *Après le deluge, moi.* Whelk OK, if you say so. Lawrence Welk: half-shell bandstand, champagne bubbles up from the briny deep. Polka dots. Wait. Are they polka dots because people who dance the polka hop around or because they like to wear dots when they do or because, aargh, the music is dotty? I hate the word *dotty*. Probably I would not like being named Dorothy. Be that as it may (O whose spirit is this for it is the spirit I do not seek), I'm still seeing dots, those awful Saturday nights when my grandparents would babysit and insist on watching old L.W. Ono. His initials are the same as mine. I was going to say I remember the lamplight of those nights—queasy and full of fake paneling, making it hard to feel any better about its being 1973, but this is too much. Or not enough. Because right before Lawrence Welk, we had to watch Wild Kingdom which was worse because, in exactly the same way as on Lawrence Welk, they would tell you what the thing you were watching meant, only now it was about animals, which you still had hopes were real.

Trading Little Trinkets with the Gods

So OK. Soak. *Souk.* Bazaar. Bizarre. Why am I—was I?—printing? I like the press of pen? Press. Press your trousers. How come some people say trousers and davenport and some people say pants and couch? This sounds like something one should have an opinion about at a dinner table where one is a newcomer and wishes she hadn't come. Just think, there is a city named Davenport, Iowa. Do you know someone there? I do. Couch, Missouri. Table, North Dakota. They start to sound like commands. Or consumer enclaves. A profit respected in such a hometown. So OK, ah so, back to soak. Soaked. Taken. Sounds like a good idea right now. Gooder than thinking about press versus iron. Both weighty. Weighty, another horrible word. Permanent, as in press. I heard someone say this: I can't wait for the future. I don't know what she meant or really where I would ever feel safe. The press of possibilities. The improbability of saying your prayers. I am yearning for you now. It's Mardi Gras. Occasional blue sparks are crossing the page.

Welling

The wand is an instrument and instruments in dreams mean what they actually are, the devices of man [sic] to concretize his will. For instance, a knife is my will to cut. —*Carl Jung*

[Interruptus—
        Do we wish to write with this pen or with this pen? One is skinnier. One is left with the question where or whether to put the question mark and with another about this now-habitual loop atop the w when it heads for an h: Whence? Why? Then there is the popping in one's neck and then the real estate agent arrives amid great squealing. Which draws one's attention to—]

We will compose a letter requesting moolah. We will churn butter later. We will wonder whether anyone else will arrive. We will attempt to have a productive day. We will describe the pine boughs as parallel llines, no, as staves of bark with the green notes climbing. We will admit a mechanical roar from the window below. We will feel and quickly suppress compassion for the grain of the table where it is exposed. We will look briefly at shoes in the room and record that Morgan's are new, Morgan's are blue. We will consider having a baby in order to have something to name. We will notice a pencil held so tenderly in a hand. The way a knife—no, no. This is the end of our willing.

Flight Path of Real Desires (my sister visits on the astral plane)

Here I am writing away and there you are shuffling your books. Except by the time I get to the end of the sentence, you aren't. What if they invent a computer with a hook-up for your brain so that whatever you thought would turn into words? No more lapse of time means no more lapse of space? *All the clouds turn to words, all the words float in sequence, no one knows what they mean, everyone just ignores them.* Please hear this Eno tune in our head, and speaking of tuning out, you are doing a good job of ignoring the stranger in our midst. Don't you wonder? Don't you think she's yours? What if she's a terrorist? What if she's the recording angel? What if she's the man from Glad? Do you even know about the man from Glad? In the future they will have advertising-dating, like carbon dating. The man from Glad, Mr. Clean, the muffin man, do you know. I always hated that tune. I felt excluded by cuteness, which may explain why I hate the Xmas carol of the little drummer boy, parumpatumtum, too. I also hate the word *patty melt* and so does the stranger in our midst who is my sister. Say it and we flinch: patty melt. See? Melts us like rain does the wicked witch, but the weather report reports more snow. More snow is to be on the grass, alas. After that, what is there to say? I hate to go back to parumpatumtum, but does anybody have any Tums? Either the flu or some toxic falafel is doing me in. Spin. No, not that please. Pedigrease. Pedicurean. Yes, in my philosophy, my feet are wet and cold. All told, my desire is toward dry socks and its angle of incidence acute.

Postcard: To my amaze

Dear who. Why dear? Why a letter? It is Valentine's Day. Let that be an answer. Or injunction: Dear so and so, I love you, be mine. Rather, Be Mine should be an exhortation or an invitation. It's certainly incorrect as command. Possession is 9/10 of the law—at least in Louisiana. Home of Tabasco and the Napoleonic code, I hasten to add, lest you think I am dumping on the South, my homeland. But of course almost everywhere has been my homeland: NM, IA, CA, NY, NC, OH, VT, AL, MS, MD, MA, ME. Maybe that makes me federal, eminent domain, I can dump where I please with impunity. Dear you, please to welcome this radioactive, dioxin-ridden junk into your water supply, and enjoy the Mardi Gras. But why would I want to? Unlike a corporation, I have a heart. Hearts—and back to the subject lately at hand, hand of cards, flush, blush (oh my dear), full house, house of the rising sun—New Orleans, yes, but no, back to my then-seven-year-old cousin, good lord I can't remember her name, oh yeah Lisa, who when we played hearts in 1972 would meditate thusly: hearts, barts, farts . . . thus anticipating both Bart Simpson and Butthead by a decade. Out of the mouths of babes.

The Laundress Maunders II

Laundromat, laundrymat, here we are again. Agayne. Imagine spelling your name Jayne. Imagine a small disaster with a red wagon is now taking place on a sidewalk near you. The boy, he says she made him break his back. Stand up and arch your back like this, is what she says to him for him to see if it is broken. He does. A cat sits on the sidewalk, watching. One ear swivels. The injured party does not cry. He bleeds from one knee. A mother is fetched, observes the bleeds. This party of three departs for the laundry, accompanied by a giant noise: wagon wheels on concrete.

A man on a motorcycle carries a green bucket. A man in a golfing hat walks with three women. Two are fat. His shirt is green. As long as I am busy telling, I can hope to be allowed to be. He told me his dream of minefields to prove being around me is like being in one. My heart and my stomach sank. One of three beer bottles on a slanty window sill falls by itself. A t-shirt tag sticks up like a tongue on the neck of a man who appears on roller blades to inspect. He puts it back up on the slanty sill. A black dog and a woman come out his door quick.

The black dog is happiest to be. Expensive white cars go by, three. Two white butterflies dance the dance of DNA. After he said I was neurotic and gave his convincing evidence, I put a deck chair in the driveway and looked at late evening clouds above the trees. A whole parakeet with its eyes closed was one feather of the wing of another. I see what this means. A cloudy tabby stretched out in mid-pounce arched above me. Better I live in the middle of nowhere and hang my laundry to dry on trees.

Wednesday Morning Pray Time

Trial. Tribulation. Psycho-sexual amputation. So busy. So big. What is happening here? O lord god in heaven save me from an uninhabitable moment. No eye contact feels safer in here. She has a bagel in her pocket. How come it's not bagle like bugle? The music of bugles is bagel-like, going round and round and coming out here. How can she but giggle at the French horn's effluence, etc. Also in evidence today that other hole in the psyche's ozone, figure of the Great Naught, Aquinas-esque estimation of the female sex as sewer, wound, Freudian source of the river of envy, poor yoni. All this, the road not taken today. Have I ignored it and has it gone away? No no row row boat, river, slipstream, ocean view, harbor home, harvest home, food bank, turkey dinner, table laden, linden the tree, linden the tea, the leap from forest canopy to golden savannah, Susanna don't you cry for me, for I've gone to Tanganyika with a thumb piano on my knee. Little Jack Horner, his corner. Thumb, plum, sex in a nutshell, plumb line, heart line, throw out the live line (phone sex) I mean lifeline, Jesus is coming for me. When he washed oh when he washed when my Jesus washed he washed my sins away. O happy day with thunder clouds, O dunderhead, O Donner, O Blitzen, all alone (a sorry pass) in the wrack of the roof of history, o tool Machiavellian, o fool antediluvian, o water well blessed, o accountant overdressed, o men, a men, women, and linen, a linnet and back to a linden, a tree (the voice says find a place to stop, stop, second hand channeling still the discourse on the watch, *the sad and happy clocks*, the pattern on his socks but actually, ouch, the big hand stopped with the tree). Bated breath on the hook of the line of communication dropped down from the otherwise empty heaven: in the beginning was the word and with it, heaven saved me.

Für Bowser

The tops of the trees look like dog tails which is a thought I do not know what to do with before a thunderstorm. A little red car honks its little tinny horn. Children wearing pastel bike helmets look like pale insect babies. My dog used to go into the kitchen and sit and look at the dishwasher whenever it thunderstormed. It did it a lot where we lived. If you can call that living. It was more like a suspension in a colloid medium. Collie-oid. Beagle-oid. My dog was neither. This, he said, is evolution, but I forget what he pointed to. Something, uncomfortably, on my person, I believe. My nose like a finch beak specialized for Alpine climes? (Or climbs?) What was the name of that mountain in my grandpa's hometown? Not the Matterhorn, I hope: glacier as Kleenex, an unhappy trope. Grosse Pointe?: no, although Raoul who hailed from there had quite the schnoz. The Nez Percé, for whom the scent of uranium tailings and copper dross were too much? Then what? No matter. As in the supposed nothingness inside us all, every atom its own vast mall. When I lie down and inquire of my left forearm how goes it, *ça va* in there, I perceive it to be happy. However, the emptiness that comes over me at the mall appalls. Space vs. spacey. Race vs. racy. Race music, thunderdome, pace car, game time, anglo hot under dogs, peace maker, cloud shaker. Soccer and ninepins in the heavens as that ole man goes rolling home: lightning means to give the dog a bone.

The Dinner Date

Just a little word, w____: someone could say it to you, and it could make every-thing different. In your soul. It could. I am ready for St. Columb and his doves, shortly after. You, he, they could be ready. Them. An us. Cleanthus, a flower. Mr. Roethke, you think like a flower, he said. Good lord, way too much cologne just sat down next to me. Hello, Mr. _____. Hello, Timmy, how is Lassie? A shaggy dog story. Don't you feel like a story? Let's talk about the 1960's. If you can, you are a story to those who were born in the 1970's. He is one of those. I am one of them. The pages turn and turn. Another arrival; who might this very late person be? A certain amount of shuffling economically. Everybody pitted against everybody—I am no force for harmony. It would seem to be not for me, the alchemical work of har—no, can't say it again. Elton John pollution. A cynical, surly, doggy vision. *I hope it is no very cynical asperity not to confess obligations where no benefit has been received.* Explaining how busy he is, sexu-ally, he gave her pedigree: five novels. (Foh: variant of faugh; an exclamation of disgust or contempt; poh; fie.) Ready or not, here comes disappointment dressed for the fashion show of silence again . . .

What when the dot dot dots leak right through the silence and the kingdom of heaven again means violence?

Boom Profits of Doom

Now it's later. Than it was. O poor hand on that man. What's its problem, do we suppose? Onward, onward, Christian soldiers, marching as to war, is what. As too far. *Far niente.* Desert Shield. Horse's ass. Asps. Larks. Tanks. Tongues in aspic. Loose lips sink ships. QE II, Lady Di, Sarajevo's only gossip: "Let them eat the border." Larder. Warder. Cannon fodder. A five-star, five-son mother: Madame, you work for the military? Mahler, polder, wooden shoes, wooden house, wooden spouse. "Lucy, I'm home." Cha cha cha, castanets, bodycast, cast of thousands, theater of operations, meet my agent, Orange, an amputee, QED. Vietnam era, sounds like *error, the truth will out with every mistake.* Hello, I'm Lowell Thomas and You Are There. I wasn't, not been there but done that several ways: when your veteran lover screams in the night, don't be afraid. Do be a Doobie, Don't be a Don'tBee. Of this and like philosophy, boys and girls, do beware. Said Simple Simon to the Pieman, "I haven't any wheres." Me either, but exile could be coming to an end here . . . Still I feel its chilly chill. But assume love, why not, what hasn't it got to do with? E.g., hey buddy gotta dime? Quarter in the sole of the shoe, money at the heart of the matter. Penny loafers. Corporate loafers, corporate ladders lead to arm and leg-adon. GE brings good things to light and—all together, now—it kills them. Good evening, ladies and gentlemen, we are proud to present *The Union Carbide Hour*, featuring your hostess with the ghostes, Gita Bhopal. Hurry up please because you know what? It's way past time.

"Under the Tinsel There Is the Real Tinsel"

And God said unto them, Be fruitful and multiply, and replenish the
earth, and subdue it.—*Genesis*

The world rests on the back of an elephant, the wise man said. And on what does the elephant
rest? I asked him. Why, the elephant rests on the back of a turtle, he answered. And on what
does the turtle rest? I asked. The turtle rests on another turtle. And on what does this other
turtle rest? I asked. He answered, It's turtles all the way down.

Here we go echoing down the walls. Why not, although halls are so evocative.
Provocative. Vocation, vacation, long-distance call girls, Thailand's best loca-
tion, Best Values In World Travel, *all creation groans in travail*, Ski Vail, stock
value, shock value, mock turtle island: Disneyfied earth adrift in Bambi blood,
turtle island unmoored. Their ancient eyes, needle claws in the toes, the idea for
paisley in yellow and green on their strange soft skins. My skins, your skins, her
skins, for "I'm Marlon Perkins and this is Wild Kingdom" (*which you still had*
hopes were real). I gave her my poems and she said, Oh goody. Perfectly mani-
cured and from New York City, kiss kiss on the cheek, her beautiful this, her
beautiful that, her turtle green eyes and her hair the color of the shadow of the
thing I wouldn't remember now: my kitten killed by the one who was to care
for it, the hand to pet the turtle's head instead to snap it off. Snapshot of A
Childhood. The horrible playground where "In the darkest Antarctica day, everybody waits to see if the big hand of great god will pet them, reach and pet
and open the starry fingers . . ." The opening of the hand, it could be something
bad in there, the worst bug you've ever seen, the heart, it could be love.

Having said that it seems I have nothing to say. I am a turtle crawling down a
carpeted hall alone.

V. TRIANGLE

Two straight lines cannot enclose a space.

—Axiom 10

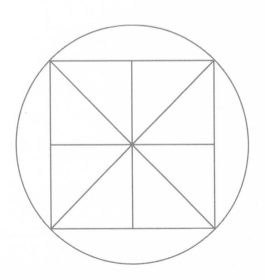

But When the Representation Does Not Do Justice to the Thought, the Meaning Is Unpleasant

I am the woman who had devils in her
And could not get them out.
Floss for the teeth *FLEECE FOR THE FLOCK* hey
Did not work.
Reflection, resolution, resignation, all earnest,
Did not work.
Then one day—
              and here she is: I am.

SURELY THE NEXT THINK I DO IS DRINK THE GREEN TEA
FROM ITS LEAVES IN MY CUP, I type with hortatory hand.

Justice is doen. Done.
            (i.e., I yam what I yam)

Wants to Sit in the Big Chair. Does.

My life, however, does not
have enough shape to be stapled.

I fell in love when she said,
"Any insect creatures' babies makes me disgusted."

For these people, they just open their mouths
and the world is there.

Whereas I have ruined too many words
already.

Dialogum

—for Peter

It has nothing to do with me
that there are no answers on that answering machine.
The cherry tree's cherries descry,
deplore, dispute disparity between
to be and to seem.
It doesn't matter to me:
I eat them.

The pink tennis shoes chews
her gum which moves
her henna'd hair. Hers
is a dream of Else and Other
wise beyond their years.
She calls them a man.
Who hears that you want him to love and can
it mean what you think he fears—
et cetera.

Et cetera. That, alone,
I'm allowed to say,
dear.

The New Age

i. Its humble beginnings

Victim is my little name.
I can tweak my own ears.

ii. Its manifesto; casual invocation of the new physics

We are all new, and electrons doing around, in order that beginnings be made.
Many of us, although dancing, are afraid to be asked to dance. Music may be
danced through to get inside of music. It is awful to be on an outside knowing
there is an inside, awful not to be in it. However, the music goes on and on,
even when you don't hear it anymore, still somewhere it is going on, perhaps
in you, electron. Why not think a consoling thought: As long as you are, you
can never not be there, the music's place. Furthermore, unlike the universe, no
strings attached, assembly not required, you don't have to stand on anything to
be there. Yet *there* is always going like a wave appears to go nowhere really. It
inhabits you, removing the no place of memory, replenishing this with the tin
and iron sounds. The tin and iron sounds, like this: low-pressure system in
Ankara heads for the temples of Angor Wat. Hear here an affliction, here hear
one long tear in the grass-green silk, plenty grasses, hard to keep track, violin
shears keep at it, jawing after silence. Whereupon our diffidence allows the
middle to go past. At last, at play in the fields of necessity: the tin and iron
sounds, given airplay in the end. O tin and iron sounds, let us begin.

iii. Its debut on Community Access TV

Not much light, and memories of other rooms with dolls in them. She says what she says for the feeling you will have of entrance and story, the long history of promise and story. She says, *I will tell you.* However, the You must be game.

She warms up with a song about flowers. Her ruined kindness the kindness of strangers: she looks herself up in the archives, makes some notes appropriate to sopranos. She is her own *other*, authoring both jessamine and Molly Bloom's recapitulated yes. Say it; she won't. *I am old.* She aims to sing some other self into being (in her debt). Nevertheless, somewhere, something is cold.

The fog rolls over the worm in the dirt it educates, which is the answer to whether it's a matter of interior weather or outer here: it's all the same to heroines and dolls. She says, *You have goddesses in you. You're a real doll.* She dictates.

"Whether tis nobler . . ." Is the ancient name of her venerable house the failure of things to null? "Outrageous fortune." Curiosity as form of anticipation. Plot vs. dispersal. The fog rolls. Dolls age. *Where has this message come from?* is what she will not ask. Reticence; pangs of limitation expressed in the language of erasure. Here, is there a danger? She tells it as a healing story. She says she is a channel.

A Calculus of Readiness

I, too, come from the city of dolls.
A small palm is my umbrella.
This takes care of above
but below, the blind river of sadness rolls
on and in it, a hand is always reaching up
to pick fish from the night-time sky.

The lines on the palm of the hand lure a trout
with a strand of hair from the head of a doll.
The bait is the hope for a hand on your brow.
Shadows play on the wall. Or the face of a doll.
The plants eyeing each other
is all.

I would not call the stars generous.
They don't cry enough for dolls to play Drink Me.
They don't cast a covenant's fishy rainbow
yet leaf faces watch the open window
where they hang far and hard.
The rein of starlight a second hand

with which to play Go Fish.
Now Give me a hand, plants. Now give me
good-night, stars.

Chez Poetess

This is the glitter world.
It costs a lot:
the trees are sick with it.

Doctor, doctor, come quick.
Here is a bad case of Pulitzer.
Lookit, a stick up the ass,
no room for thermometer.
You'll have to guess
at the temperature
of a star, a thing
the star will think
you should naturally know.

The stink, at least, is natural.
Venus, the evening star,
really a ball of gasses.
Polyvinylchlorides, dioxins.
Hungry masses?
Let them kiss asses.
I bin to italy
I bin to france
I seen the emperor's
new underpants.

And I glitter.
I cost a lot.
I'm a trick, I'm a john,
I'm a date with the money
to pencil in destiny

later for dinner.
Let them eat what I forsake—
they'd look better thinner.

Doctor, doctor, will s/he live?
Poor stick, such a life,
what a stench. Shtick,
Schick, a very straight razor.
Try laser for a very straight face.
Deforestation progresses apace.
Stuck up but never
out on a limb—
it's the fashion
in this very special place.

The Upper Class

For three days the trees
held their breath.

You could see it:
a crystal sheath.

The soul's effluence
become its showcase—

please do not lean
on the glass of progress—

borrows suffering's gravity
to underline its worth,

as if to say (icily)
my very pestilence is wealth.

High Culture

Cumulous on the glass of the sky, on
the inside. The circumference is etched.
Tremulous, the surface—a bluebottle
suddenly flies. A hedge, I bet.

This unexpected flight cracks a glass
in the house Jack never built, a labor of guilt.
On the streets of heaven, barefoot
but dressed to the hilt.

Wednesdays, the Ladies Club joins them.
A cloud slips. A lady adjusts
the hem of her skirt:
slips should not show.

When they do, you're a slut
and the leaves of the hedge

rustle.

Misses Coordinates (old world mail order)

We lived in a map of the world
and we knew it. It was
all right with us.

We could require a robe of hemisphere,
the Fall collection of mid-size seas,
breathe haute-inspired atmospheres

in the fitting room where
one is always the other in disguise.

All this, if dislocating for others,
was very fine for us.

The Scientific Method

i. Notebook

Belief like hell can affect you & how you behave
Perception; influenced by emotion
Is how world seems when depressed real?
Need many views to get accurate picture
How to know what reality is?
Things are like other things and so can be mistaken

ii. Observation

I thought the professor in the next room
said when I walked into this one,
"Think about madness." "Think about madness,"
he said again as I sat and then
I realized he was saying magnets;
this is the engineering building.

iii. Interrogation and conclusion

Should that semi-colon be a colon?
Baconian, in a pig's eye.

Radioactive Assay and Epitaph (Indian School)

. . . so the secrets of nature betray themselves more readily when tormented.
—Francis Bacon, *Novum Organum*

The way paved with iron of interdicted sites;
the face, sudden, of the world revealed
on which we read nothing
more than aversion—

Total immersion
in our corruption
brought about extinction: its own
language forbidden, the world learned Bacon's.

Witness

I saw that a star had broken its rope
in the stables of heaven—

This homeless one will find her home
in the foothills of a green century.

Who sleeps beside still waters, wakes.
The terrestrial hands of the heaven clock

comb out the comet's tangled mane
and twelve strands float free.

In the absence of light and gravity,
slowly as dust, or the continents' drift,

sinuous, they twine a text,
one letter to an eon:

I am the dawn horse.
Ride me.

vi. POINT

We will only observe that the ideas which correspond to the words point, line, and surface do not admit of such definitions as will really supply the ideas to a person who is destitute of them. The so-called definitions may be regarded as cautions.

—I. Todhunter

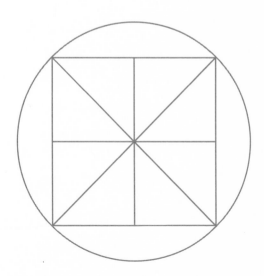

Sufficient Causes and Artifacts

i. For the voice to cry, All flesh is grass

    a. After Elixir comes Elizabethan,
    née *Kyrie* elision . . .

    b. In 1678, she went to Worms
    to the colloquy there about religion . . .

    a. (. . . and with vinegar affords
    a crust of verdigris.)

    b. (. . . and loses, though but verbal
    her precipitate reward.)

ii. On which hang all the spawn and the prophets

    She has eyebrows like tadpoles. Don't forget.
    If you do, the frog prince will, too
    And our world will fall apart backwards.

iii. For the tiny ignition to occur

    In physics, Epicurus was an atomist
    of the school of Democritus.

Foh. [Exclamation of . . . *remember me,*
remember me . . .]

(I don't like anyone telling me nothing,
forgive me.)

Apparently, I wrote all the addresses
with ink that paled and disappeared.

My desk is white like a page afraid
of such correspondence.

for we all do fade as a leaf

Notes

The definitions, axioms, and postulates here are Thomas L. Heath's translation from Euclid's Greek.

Ear Rational: "After the final no . . ." is from Wallace Stevens's "The Well Dressed Man with a Beard."

Of Unknowing Again: "we have a beautiful cosmos . . ." is an Ivor Cutler lyric.

"'Under the Tinsel There Is the Real Tinsel'": The title comes from Madonna on a talk show; "In the darkest Antarctica day . . ." is from a Lynda Barry cartoon.

THE IOWA POETRY PRIZE & EDWIN FORD PIPER POETRY AWARD WINNERS

1987
Elton Glaser, *Tropical Depressions*
Michael Pettit, *Cardinal Points*

1988
Bill Knott, *Outremer*
Mary Ruefle, *The Adamant*

1989
Conrad Hilberry, *Sorting the Smoke*
Terese Svoboda, *Laughing Africa*

1990
Philip Dacey,
    Night Shift at the Crucifix Factory
Lynda Hull, *Star Ledger*

1991
Greg Pape, *Sunflower Facing the Sun*
Walter Pavlich,
    Running near the End of the World

1992
Lola Haskins, *Hunger*
Katherine Soniat, *A Shared Life*

1993
Tom Andrews,
    The Hemophiliac's Motorcycle
Michael Heffernan, *Love's Answer*
John Wood, *In Primary Light*

1994
James McKean, *Tree of Heaven*
Bin Ramke, *Massacre of the Innocents*
Ed Roberson,
    Voices Cast Out to Talk Us In

1995
Ralph Burns, *Swamp Candles*
Maureen Seaton, *Furious Cooking*

1996
Pamela Alexander, *Inland*
Gary Gildner,
    The Bunker in the Parsley Fields
John Wood,
    The Gates of the Elect Kingdom

1997
Brendan Galvin, *Hotel Malabar*
Leslie Ullman, *Slow Work through Sand*

1998
Kathleen Peirce, *The Oval Hour*
Bin Ramke, *Wake*
Cole Swensen, *Try*

1999
Larissa Szporluk, *Isolato*
Liz Waldner,
    A Point Is That Which Has No Part